MW00976851

THIS BOOK BELONGS TO

_____

START DATE

_____

SHE READS TRUTH

EXECUTIVE

FOUNDER/CHIEF EXECUTIVE OFFICER
Raechel Myers

CO-FOUNDER/CHIEF CONTENT OFFICER
Amanda Bible Williams

CHIEF OPERATING OFFICER
Ryan Myers

EXECUTIVE ASSISTANT
Sarah Andereck

EDITORIAL

EDITORIAL DIRECTOR
Jessica Lamb

CONTENT EDITOR
Kara Gause

ASSOCIATE EDITORS
Bailey Gillespie
Ellen Taylor
Tameshia Williams

EDITORIAL ASSISTANT
Hannah Little

CREATIVE

CREATIVE DIRECTOR
Jeremy Mitchell

LEAD DESIGNER
Kelsea Allen

DESIGNERS
Abbey Benson
Davis DeLisi
Annie Glover

MARKETING

MARKETING DIRECTOR
Krista Juline Williams

MARKETING MANAGER
Katie Matuska Pierce

SOCIAL MEDIA MANAGER
Ansley Rushing

COMMUNITY SUPPORT SPECIALIST
Margot Williams

SHIPPING & LOGISTICS

LOGISTICS MANAGER
Lauren Gloyne

SHIPPING MANAGER
Sydney Bess

CUSTOMER SUPPORT SPECIALIST
Katy McKnight

FULFILLMENT SPECIALISTS
Abigail Achord
Cait Baggerman
Kamiren Passavanti

SUBSCRIPTION INQUIRIES
orders@shereadstruth.com

CONTRIBUTORS

PHOTOGRAPHY
Tchaizel Ambion (24, 32, 40, 52, 60)
Tess Pereyo (44)

@SHEREADSTRUTH

Download the
She Reads Truth app,
available for iOS
and Android

Subscribe to the
She Reads Truth podcast

SHEREADSTRUTH.COM

SHE READS TRUTH™

© 2020 by She Reads Truth, LLC

All rights reserved.

All photography used by permission.

ISBN 978-1-952670-10-7

1 2 3 4 5 6 7 8 9 10

No part of this publication may be reproduced, distributed, or transmitted in any form or by any means, including photocopying, recording, or other electronic or mechanical methods, without the prior written permission of She Reads Truth, LLC, except in the case of brief quotations embodied in critical reviews and certain other noncommercial uses permitted by copyright law.

All Scripture is taken from the Christian Standard Bible®. Copyright © 2020 by Holman Bible Publishers. Used by permission. Christian Standard Bible® and CSB® are federally registered trademarks of Holman Bible Publishers.

Research support provided by Logos Bible Software™. Learn more at logos.com.

Though the dates in this book have been carefully researched, scholars disagree on the dating of many biblical events.

This book was printed offset in Nashville, Tennessee, on 70# Lynx Opaque. Cover is 100# Cougar Opaque with a soft touch lamination and Infinity Foil #75.

ESTHER

SHE READS TRUTH

GOD'S NAME DOES NOT HAVE TO BE MENTIONED IN ORDER FOR HIS PRESENCE TO BE FELT, FOR HIS WILL TO BE ACCOMPLISHED, AND FOR HIS LOVINGKINDNESS TO BE EVIDENT.

Raechel Myers
FOUNDER & CHIEF
EXECUTIVE OFFICER

The book of Esther is about God. While His name is never mentioned, His masterful, sustaining, promise-keeping, unseen hand is at work throughout. God's name does not have to be mentioned in order for His presence to be felt, for His will to be accomplished, and for His lovingkindness to be evident.

Likewise, my story and yours are also about God. Were a community of women to read our stories thousands of years from now, God's steadfast loving kindness would be the theme, whether or not we acknowledge Him or even speak His name.

Esther is one of my favorite books of the Bible because the narrative storytelling is downright delightful. There are twists and turns and (spoiler alert!) the good guys win, the bad guy gets hung on his own gallows, an unlikley girl is invited to play a pivotal role in God's great rescue plan, and the persistent uncle gets a parade thrown in his honor. In the end, one of the major festivals on the Jewish calendar is instituted to commemorate the preserving hand of the not-mentioned God of Israel. The book of Esther reads like a play, both a comedy and a drama, yet it is the true historical account of a volatile time in world history.

Over the course of this reading plan, we'll read the story of a woman who gained the favor of the king of Persia because she "had a beautiful figure and was extremely good-looking" (Esther 2:7). But as we dig deeper, we'll see that God's rescue plan was not about Esther's beauty or even her bravery, but about God's faithfulness. Esther had the favor of the true King, not because of any service she could provide but simply because God keeps His promises to His people.

Along with the daily Scripture readings in this Study Book, we've included some fantastic extra features, including my favorite, "Reversals in Esther" on page 36. (It makes me fist pump in the air when I read about God's justice and sense of humor!) The daily reflection questions can lead to interesting conversation, making this study a great one to read with friends.

The book of Esther is about God. His hand is visible in every plot twist and moment of reversal and redemption. As you read over the next two weeks, we pray this story of rescue will challenge and enlarge the way you see your own life against the strong and loving hands of our Creator and Sustainer—the God who is at work in your story as well.

Long live the King!

DESIGN ON PURPOSE

At She Reads Truth, we believe in pairing the inherently beautiful Word of God with the aesthetic beauty it deserves. Each of our resources is thoughtfully and artfully designed to highlight the beauty, goodness, and truth of Scripture in a way that reflects the themes of each curated reading plan.

For this Study Book, we chose a purple color palette to represent the royal setting and characters within the book of Esther. We also reversed the typeface as a design feature throughout, reflecting the many reversals of fortune in this Old Testament story. Did you spot the crown created from the "R"s on the cover?

These artistic elements remind us that God is always at work, often in unseen and unexpected ways.

ARTEMIS

ABCDEFGHIJKLMN
OPQRSTUVWXYZ

ABCDEFGHIJKLM
NOPQRSTUVWXYZ

1234567890

GOTHAM · MEDIUM

abcdefghijklmn
opqrstuvwxyz

PANTONE
524 U

PANTONE
1955 U

75
infinityfoils.com

PANTONE
720 U

HOW TO USE THIS BOOK

She Reads Truth is a community of women dedicated
to reading the Word of God every day. The Bible is
living and active, and we confidently hold it higher
than anything we can do or say.

READ & REFLECT

This **Esther** Study Book focuses
primarily on Scripture, with bonus
resources to facilitate deeper
engagement with God's Word.

SCRIPTURE READING

Designed for a Monday start,
this Study Book presents the
book of Esther in daily readings,
with supplemental passages for
additional context.

REFLECTION QUESTIONS

Each weekday also features
questions and note-taking space
for personal reflection.

COMMUNITY & CONVERSATION

Join women from Honolulu to Hong Kong as
they read Truth with you!

 ## SHE READS TRUTH APP

Devotionals corresponding to each daily reading can
be found in the **Esther** reading plan on the She Reads
Truth app. You can also participate in community
discussions, download free lock screens for Weekly
Truth memorization, and more.

GRACE DAY

Use Saturdays to catch up on your reading, pray, and rest in the presence of the Lord.

WEEKLY TRUTH

Sundays are set aside for Scripture memorization.

EXTRAS

This book features additional tools to help you gain a deeper understanding of the text.

See a complete list of extras on the following page.

SHEREADSTRUTH.COM

All of our reading plans and devotionals are also available at SheReadsTruth.com. Invite your family, friends, and neighbors to read along with you!

SHE READS TRUTH PODCAST

Join our She Reads Truth founders and their guests each Monday as they open their Bibles and talk about the beauty, goodness, and truth they find there. Subscribe to the podcast so you don't miss conversations about the current commmunity reading plan.

TABLE OF
CONTENTS

EXTRAS

She Reads Esther
12

How to Read Historical Narrative in the Bible
14

Key People in the Book of Esther
16

Timeline: The Book of Esther in Biblical History
26

Reversals in Esther
36

Spiritual Rhythms in the Book of Esther
50

Old Testament Festivals Fulfilled in Christ
68

For the Record
80

1

2

DAY 1   The King's Decree   18

DAY 2   Esther Becomes Queen   22

DAY 3   Haman Plans to Kill the Jews   28

DAY 4   Mordecai Appeals to Esther   32

DAY 5   Esther Approaches the King   38

DAY 6   Grace Day   42

DAY 7   Weekly Truth   44

DAY 8   Mordecai Honored by the King   46

DAY 9   Haman Is Executed   52

DAY 10   Esther Intervenes for the Jews   56

DAY 11   The Victories of the Jews   60

DAY 12   Mordecai's Fame   64

DAY 13   Grace Day   70

DAY 14   Weekly Truth   72

SHE READS ESTHER

SHE READS ESTHER

ON THE TIMELINE

The story of Esther is rooted in the historical account of King Ahasuerus, who ruled Persia from 486 to 465 BC. Esther was made queen of Persia in approximately 479 BC, Haman's plot to destroy the Jewish people occurred in 474 BC, and the first celebration of Purim took place in 473 BC. The events in Esther occurred before the events of Nehemiah but after the Decree of Cyrus allowed the Jewish people in exile to return to Jerusalem. Most likely the book was written in the fourth century BC with Mordecai as its author.

A LITTLE BACKGROUND

Esther is a unique book. It never mentions God by name, although His presence is implied in Mordecai's allusion to divine providence (4:14). The book of Esther recounts specific historical events, yet it is also a piece of literature, a narrative with all of the literary features necessary to make a great story. Its purposes are not always explicitly stated but are derived from the story as a whole.

MESSAGE & PURPOSE

For the Jewish people scattered around the Persian Empire, the book of Esther was a story that gave encouragement and hope. It provided a model of how Jewish people could not only survive but thrive in a Gentile environment. It displayed the work of God, evident but unseen, in the unfolding story of deliverance and redemption—making an orphan girl the queen and using her courage and influence to save the Jewish people from annihilation.

GIVE THANKS FOR THE BOOK OF ESTHER

The book of Esther teaches us about God's providence. God's promise to give the Jewish people an eternal ruler still stood, even in the face of threatened annihilation. Without ever mentioning Him by name, the book of Esther underscores the Lord's presence and sovereignty in the lives of His people. God's invisible hand was always at work in the story of Esther and her people, securing their deliverance even before Haman sought to devise their destruction.

HOW TO READ

Historical Narrative in the Bible

Esther is one of twelve Historical Books in the Old Testament. These twelve books present in narrative form the true account of God's relationship with the people of Israel, from their entry into the promised land to their exile and return. The following page includes some helpful tips to remember when reading Esther and other historical narratives in the Bible.

© 2020 She Reads Truth. All rights reserved.

HISTORICAL NARRATIVE IS ALSO THEOLOGICAL HISTORY, WRITTEN TO SHOW HOW GOD WORKS IN AND THROUGH HISTORICAL EVENTS. Historical narrative in the Bible records true events, but was written to do more than just document history.

BIBLICAL NARRATIVE IS OFTEN DESCRIPTIVE RATHER THAN PRESCRIPTIVE. The examples of people's choices are not always positive or meant to be followed.

OUR SOCIAL NORMS ARE DIFFERENT THAN THOSE WE ENCOUNTER IN THE BIBLE. God spoke into culture as it existed. It is important to keep in mind that not all practices found in Scripture (e.g., polygamy or slavery) were part of God's design for His creation. At the same time, we remember that though human laws and customs vary over time, eternal truths remain unchanged.

GOD'S REVELATION IS GRADUAL. Since we have the complete Old and New Testaments, we benefit from knowledge about certain aspects of God's plan that the people we read about in the Old Testament did not.

THE BIBLE WAS WRITTEN BY PEOPLE LIVING IN THE MIDDLE OF REDEMPTION HISTORY. What they wrote was often selected to explain the circumstances God's people were experiencing in their own day.

PEOPLE IN THE BIBLE ARE COMPLEX and rarely fall into neat categories of "good" and "bad." Jesus is the only one who is truly good.

GOD WORKED THROUGH BROKEN, SINFUL PEOPLE in the Bible, and He still does.

Key People in the Book of Esther

From dramatic plot twists to seemingly impossible odds, Esther is a compelling read by any standard. Here is an overview of the key people in this Old Testament narrative, and the reference for their first appearance in the book.

Ahasuerus
ESTHER 1:1

King of 127 provinces from India to Cush

Reigned in the fortress of Persia at Susa

Queen Vashti
ESTHER 1:9

King Ahasuerus's wife

Banished from the king's presence because she refused to come when he called for her

Harbona
ESTHER 1:10

One of King Ahasuerus's eunuchs

Advised the king to hang Haman on Haman's own gallows

Memucan
ESTHER 1:14

An official of Persia and Media

Advised Ahasuerus to find a new queen to replace Vashti

Hegai
ESTHER 2:3

One of King Ahasuerus's eunuchs

Placed in charge of the women who were candidates to become the new queen

© 2020 She Reads Truth. All rights reserved.

Mordecai

ESTHER 2:5

Esther's cousin and guardian who advised her to keep her ethnicity and family background a secret

Refused to bow down to Haman

Esther

ESTHER 2:7

A young Jewish girl chosen by King Ahasuerus to replace Vashti as queen

Kept her Jewish heritage a secret, then used her status as queen to save her people

Bigthan & Teresh

ESTHER 2:21

Two of King Ahasuerus's eunuchs who conspired to assassinate him

Exposed by Mordecai, who told Esther of their conspiracy

Haman

ESTHER 3:1

King Ahasuerus's highest-ranking official

Ordered all Jews to be destroyed after Mordecai refused to bow to him

Hathach

ESTHER 4:5

The king's eunuch assigned to tend to Queen Esther

Carried messages between Esther and Mordecai

Zeresh

ESTHER 5:10

Haman's wife

Advised Haman to build 75-foot gallows on which to hang Mordecai

THE KING'S DECREE

DAY

ONE

THE KING'S DECREE

Esther 1
VASHTI ANGERS THE KING

[1] These events took place during the days of Ahasuerus, who ruled 127 provinces from India to Cush. [2] In those days King Ahasuerus reigned from his royal throne in the fortress at Susa. [3] He held a feast in the third year of his reign for all his officials and staff, the army of Persia and Media, the nobles, and the officials from the provinces. [4] He displayed the glorious wealth of his kingdom and the magnificent splendor of his greatness for a total of 180 days.

[5] At the end of this time, the king held a week-long banquet in the garden courtyard of the royal palace for all the people, from the greatest to the least, who were present in the fortress of Susa. [6] White and blue linen hangings were fastened with fine white and purple linen cords to silver rods on marble columns. Gold and silver couches were arranged on a mosaic pavement of red feldspar, marble, mother-of-pearl, and precious stones.

[7] Drinks were served in an array of gold goblets, each with a different design. Royal wine flowed freely, according to the king's bounty. [8] The drinking was according to royal decree: "There are no restrictions." The king had ordered every wine steward in his household to serve whatever each person wanted. [9] Queen Vashti also gave a feast for the women of King Ahasuerus's palace.

[10] On the seventh day, when the king was feeling good from the wine, Ahasuerus commanded Mehuman, Biztha, Harbona, Bigtha, Abagtha, Zethar, and Carkas— the seven eunuchs who personally served him— [11] to bring Queen Vashti before him with her royal crown. He wanted to show off her beauty to the people and the officials, because she was very beautiful. [12] But Queen Vashti refused to come at the king's command that was delivered by his eunuchs. The king became furious and his anger burned within him.

THE KING'S DECREE

[13] The king consulted the wise men who understood the times, for it was his normal procedure to confer with experts in law and justice. [14] The most trusted ones were Carshena, Shethar, Admatha, Tarshish, Meres, Marsena, and Memucan.

They were the seven officials of Persia and Media who had personal access to the king and occupied the highest positions in the kingdom. ¹⁵ The king asked, "According to the law, what should be done with Queen Vashti, since she refused to obey King Ahasuerus's command that was delivered by the eunuchs?"

¹⁶ Memucan said in the presence of the king and his officials, "Queen Vashti has wronged not only the king, but all the officials and the peoples who are in every one of King Ahasuerus's provinces. ¹⁷ For the queen's action will become public knowledge to all the women and cause them to despise their husbands and say, 'King Ahasuerus ordered Queen Vashti brought before him, but she did not come.' ¹⁸ Before this day is over, the noble women of Persia and Media who hear about the queen's act will say the same thing to all the king's officials, resulting in more contempt and fury.

¹⁹ "If it meets the king's approval, he should personally issue a royal decree. Let it be recorded in the laws of the Persians and the Medes, so that it cannot be revoked: Vashti is not to enter King Ahasuerus's presence, and her royal position is to be given to another woman who is more worthy than she. ²⁰ The decree the king issues will be heard throughout his vast kingdom, so all women will honor their husbands, from the greatest to the least."

²¹ The king and his counselors approved the proposal, and he followed Memucan's advice. ²² He sent letters to all the royal provinces, to each province in its own script and to each ethnic group in its own language, that every man should be master of his own house and speak in the language of his own people.

PSALM 32:7-11
⁷ You are my hiding place;
you protect me from trouble.
You surround me with joyful shouts of deliverance.   *Selah*

⁸ I will instruct you and show you the way to go;
with my eye on you, I will give counsel.
⁹ Do not be like a horse or mule,
without understanding,
that must be controlled with bit and bridle
or else it will not come near you.

¹⁰ Many pains come to the wicked,
but the one who trusts in the LORD
will have faithful love surrounding him.
¹¹ Be glad in the LORD and rejoice,
you righteous ones;
shout for joy,
all you upright in heart.

PROVERBS 19:12
A king's rage is like the roaring of a lion,
but his favor is like dew on the grass.

1

REFLECTION QUESTIONS

◇ What reversals
of fortune or
"coincidences" occur
in today's reading?

◇ How was God
at work in
these events?

◇ When you look
back over your
life before you
came to faith in
Jesus, where do
you see God at
work? Write a
prayer asking God
to help you see
His presence and
provision in
your past.

ESTHER BECOMES QUEEN

ESTHER 2
THE SEARCH FOR A NEW QUEEN

¹ Some time later, when King Ahasuerus's rage had cooled down, he remembered Vashti, what she had done, and what was decided against her. ² The king's personal attendants suggested, "Let a search be made for beautiful young virgins for the king. ³ Let the king appoint commissioners in each province of his kingdom, so that they may gather all the beautiful young virgins to the harem at the fortress of Susa. Put them under the supervision of Hegai, the king's eunuch, keeper of the women, and give them the required beauty treatments. ⁴ Then the young woman who pleases the king will become queen instead of Vashti." This suggestion pleased the king, and he did accordingly.

⁵ In the fortress of Susa, there was a Jewish man named Mordecai son of Jair, son of Shimei, son of Kish, a Benjaminite. ⁶ Kish had been taken into exile from Jerusalem with the other captives when King Nebuchadnezzar of Babylon took King Jeconiah of Judah into exile. ⁷ Mordecai was the legal guardian of his cousin Hadassah (that is, Esther), because she had no father or mother. The young woman had a beautiful figure and was extremely good-looking. When her father and mother died, Mordecai had adopted her as his own daughter.

⁸ When the king's command and edict became public knowledge and when many young women were gathered at the fortress of Susa under Hegai's supervision, Esther was taken to the palace, into the supervision of Hegai, keeper of the women. ⁹ The young woman pleased him and gained his favor so that he accelerated the process of the beauty treatments and the special diet that she received. He assigned seven hand-picked female servants to her from the palace and transferred her and her servants to the harem's best quarters.

¹⁰ Esther did not reveal her ethnicity or her family background, because Mordecai had ordered her not to make them known. ¹¹ Every day Mordecai took a walk in front of the harem's courtyard to learn how Esther was doing and to see what was happening to her.

¹² During the year before each young woman's turn to go to King Ahasuerus, the harem regulation required her to receive beauty treatments with oil of myrrh for six months and then with perfumes and cosmetics for another six months. ¹³ When the young woman would go to the king, she was given whatever she requested to take with her from the harem to the palace. ¹⁴ She would go in the evening, and in the morning she would return to a second harem under the supervision of the king's eunuch Shaashgaz, keeper of the concubines. She never went to the king again, unless he desired her and summoned her by name.

ESTHER BECOMES QUEEN

¹⁵ Esther was the daughter of Abihail, the uncle of Mordecai who had adopted her as his own daughter. When her turn came to go to the king, she did not ask for anything except what Hegai, the king's eunuch, keeper of the women, suggested. Esther gained favor in the eyes of everyone who saw her.

16 She was taken to King Ahasuerus in the palace in the tenth month, the month Tebeth, in the seventh year of his reign. 17 The king loved Esther more than all the other women. She won more favor and approval from him than did any of the other virgins. He placed the royal crown on her head and made her queen in place of Vashti. 18 The king held a great banquet for all his officials and staff. It was Esther's banquet. He freed his provinces from tax payments and gave gifts worthy of the king's bounty.

MORDECAI SAVES THE KING

19 When the virgins were gathered a second time, Mordecai was sitting at the King's Gate. 20 Esther still did not reveal her family background or her ethnicity, as Mordecai had directed. She obeyed Mordecai's orders, as she always had while he raised her.

21 During those days while Mordecai was sitting at the King's Gate, Bigthan and Teresh, two of the king's eunuchs who guarded the entrance, became infuriated and planned to assassinate King Ahasuerus. 22 When Mordecai learned of the plot, he reported it to Queen Esther, and she told the king on Mordecai's behalf. 23 When the report was investigated and verified, both men were hanged on the gallows. This event was recorded in the Historical Record in the king's presence.

Proverbs 31:10–31
IN PRAISE OF A WIFE OF NOBLE CHARACTER

10 Who can find a wife of noble character?

SHE IS FAR MORE PRECIOUS THAN JEWELS.

11 The heart of her husband trusts in her,
and he will not lack anything good.
12 She rewards him with good, not evil,
all the days of her life.
13 She selects wool and flax
and works with willing hands.
14 She is like the merchant ships,
bringing her food from far away.
15 She rises while it is still night
and provides food for her household
and portions for her female servants.
16 She evaluates a field and buys it;
she plants a vineyard with her earnings.
17 She draws on her strength
and reveals that her arms are strong.
18 She sees that her profits are good,
and her lamp never goes out at night.
19 She extends her hands to the spinning staff,
and her hands hold the spindle.
20 Her hands reach out to the poor,
and she extends her hands to the needy.
21 She is not afraid for her household when it snows,
for all in her household are doubly clothed.
22 She makes her own bed coverings;
her clothing is fine linen and purple.
23 Her husband is known at the city gates,
where he sits among the elders of the land.
24 She makes and sells linen garments;
she delivers belts to the merchants.
25 Strength and honor are her clothing,
and she can laugh at the time to come.
26 Her mouth speaks wisdom,
and loving instruction is on her tongue.
27 She watches over the activities of her household
and is never idle.
28 Her children rise up and call her blessed;
her husband also praises her:
29 "Many women have done noble deeds,
but you surpass them all!"
30 Charm is deceptive and beauty is fleeting,
but a woman who fears the Lord will be praised.
31 Give her the reward of her labor,
and let her works praise her at the city gates.

2

REFLECTION QUESTIONS

◇ What reversals of fortune or "coincidences" occur in today's reading?

◇ How was God at work in these events?

◇ When you look back over the way you came to know Christ, where do you see God at work? Write a prayer asking God to help you see His presence and provision in your faith.

TIMELINE:

THE BOOK OF ESTHER
IN BIBLICAL HISTORY

Considering Esther in light of the whole story of Scripture, we are reminded that God's hand is at work even when His name is not mentioned. This timeline presents key dates in the book of Esther in the context of biblical history.

600 BC

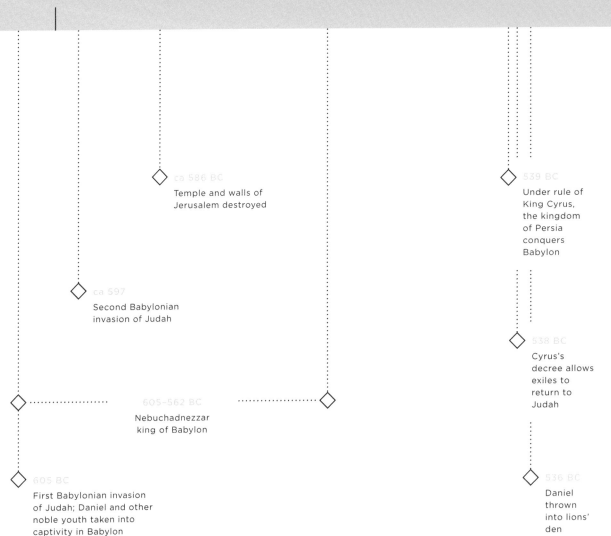

ca 586 BC
Temple and walls of Jerusalem destroyed

539 BC
Under rule of King Cyrus, the kingdom of Persia conquers Babylon

ca 597
Second Babylonian invasion of Judah

605–562 BC
Nebuchadnezzar king of Babylon

538 BC
Cyrus's decree allows exiles to return to Judah

605 BC
First Babylonian invasion of Judah; Daniel and other noble youth taken into captivity in Babylon

536 BC
Daniel thrown into lions' den

500 BC

© 2020 She Reads Truth. All rights reserved.

ca 515 BC
King Darius issues a decree that allows the Jewish people to finish building the temple without interruption

474 BC
Mordecai refuses to bow to Haman

Haman issues royal decree for annihilating the Jewish people in the Persian Empire

Esther intercedes with King Ahasuerus on behalf of her people

King Ahasuerus honors Mordecai and has Haman hanged

458 BC
Artaxerxes I issues a decree that allows exiles living in Persia to return home to Judah

Nehemiah remains in Persia, eventually becoming the royal cupbearer for King Artaxerxes

473 BC
Celebration of Purim begins

479 BC
Esther becomes queen of Persia

444 BC
While serving Susa, Nehemiah asks King Artaxerxes to allow him to return to Jerusalem to repair its walls and gates

478 BC
Mordecai thwarts Bigthan's and Teresh's conspiracy to kill King Ahasuerus

483 BC
King Ahasuerus kicks off his 180-day feast

Queen Vashti dethroned

DAY THREE

Haman plans to
kill the jews

Haman plans to
kill the jews

Esther 3

HAMAN'S PLAN TO KILL THE JEWS

¹ After all this took place, King Ahasuerus honored Haman, son of Hammedatha the Agagite. He promoted him in rank and gave him a higher position than all the other officials. ² The entire royal staff at the King's Gate bowed down and paid homage to Haman, because the king had commanded this to be done for him. But Mordecai would not bow down or pay homage. ³ The members of the royal staff at the King's Gate asked Mordecai, "Why are you disobeying the king's command?" ⁴ When they had warned him day after day and he still would not listen to them, they told Haman in order to see if Mordecai's actions would be tolerated, since he had told them he was a Jew.

⁵ When Haman saw that Mordecai was not bowing down or paying him homage, he was filled with rage. ⁶ And when he learned of Mordecai's ethnic identity, it seemed repugnant to Haman to do away with Mordecai alone. He planned to destroy all of Mordecai's people, the Jews, throughout Ahasuerus's kingdom.

⁷ In the first month, the month of Nisan, in King Ahasuerus's twelfth year, the pur—that is, the lot—was cast before Haman for each day in each month, and it fell on the twelfth month, the month Adar. ⁸ Then Haman informed King Ahasuerus, "There is one ethnic group, scattered throughout the peoples in every province of your kingdom, keeping themselves separate. Their laws are different from everyone else's and they do not obey the king's laws. It is not in the king's best interest to tolerate them. ⁹ If the king approves, let an order be drawn up authorizing their destruction, and I will pay 375 tons of silver to the officials for deposit in the royal treasury."

144,000

¹⁰ The king removed his signet ring from his hand and gave it to Haman son of Hammedatha the Agagite, the enemy of the Jews. ¹¹ Then the king told Haman, "The money and people are given to you to do with as you see fit."

¹² The royal scribes were summoned on the thirteenth day of the first month, and the order was written exactly as Haman commanded. It was intended for the royal satraps, the governors of each of the provinces, and the officials of each ethnic group and written for each province in its own script and to each ethnic group in its own language. It was written in the name of King Ahasuerus and sealed with the royal signet ring. ¹³ Letters were sent by couriers to each of the royal provinces telling the officials to destroy, kill, and annihilate all the Jewish people—young and old, women and children—and plunder their possessions on a single day, the thirteenth day of Adar, the twelfth month.

¹⁴ A copy of the text, issued as law throughout every province, was distributed to all the peoples so that they might get ready for that day. ¹⁵ The couriers left, spurred on by royal command, and the law was issued in the fortress of Susa. The king and Haman sat down to drink, while the city of Susa was in confusion.

PSALM 68:1-10, 20
GOD'S MAJESTIC POWER

For the choir director. A psalm of David. A song.

¹ God arises. His enemies scatter,
and those who hate him flee from his presence.
² As smoke is blown away,
so you blow them away.
As wax melts before the fire,
so the wicked are destroyed before God.
³ But the righteous are glad;
they rejoice before God and celebrate with joy.

⁴ Sing to God! Sing praises to his name.
Exalt him who rides on the clouds—
his name is the Lord—and celebrate before him.
⁵ God in his holy dwelling is
a father of the fatherless
and a champion of widows.
⁶ God provides homes for those who are deserted.
He leads out the prisoners to prosperity,
but the rebellious live in a scorched land.

⁷ God, when you went out before your people,
when you marched through the desert,   *Selah*
⁸ the earth trembled and the skies poured rain
before God, the God of Sinai,
before God, the God of Israel.

⁹ You, God, showered abundant rain;
you revived your inheritance when it languished.
¹⁰ Your people settled in it;
God, you provided for the poor by your goodness.

…

²⁰ OUR GOD IS A GOD OF SALVATION, AND ESCAPE FROM DEATH BELONGS TO THE LORD MY LORD.

PROVERBS 16:33
The lot is cast into the lap,
but its every decision is from the Lord.

3

REFLECTION QUESTIONS

◇ What reversals of fortune or "coincidences" occur in today's reading?

◇ How was God at work in these events?

◇ When you look at your current circumstances, where do you see God at work? Write a prayer asking God to help you see His presence and provision in your circumstances.

DAY FOUR

Mordecai Appeals to Esther

◇   ◇   ◇   ◇   ◇   ◇

ESTHER 4
MORDECAI APPEALS TO ESTHER

¹ When Mordecai learned all that had occurred, he tore his clothes, put on sackcloth and ashes, went into the middle of the city, and cried loudly and bitterly. ² He went only as far as the King's Gate, since the law prohibited anyone wearing sackcloth from entering the King's Gate. ³ There was great mourning among the Jewish people in every province where the king's command and edict reached. They fasted, wept, and lamented, and many lay in sackcloth and ashes.

⁴ Esther's female servants and her eunuchs came and reported the news to her, and the queen was overcome with fear. She sent clothes for Mordecai to wear so that he would take off his sackcloth, but he did not accept them. ⁵ Esther summoned Hathach, one of the king's eunuchs who attended her, and dispatched him to Mordecai to learn what he was doing and why. ⁶ So Hathach went out to Mordecai in the city square in front of the King's Gate. ⁷ Mordecai told him everything that had happened as well as the exact amount of money Haman had promised to pay the royal treasury for the slaughter of the Jews.

⁸ Mordecai also gave him a copy of the written decree issued in Susa ordering their destruction, so that Hathach might show it to Esther, explain it to her, and command her to approach the king, implore his favor, and plead with him personally for her people. ⁹ Hathach came and repeated Mordecai's response to Esther.

¹⁰ Esther spoke to Hathach and commanded him to tell Mordecai, ¹¹ "All the royal officials and the people of the royal provinces know that one law applies to every man or woman who approaches the king in the inner courtyard and who has not been summoned—the death penalty—unless the king extends the gold scepter, allowing that person to live. I have not been summoned to appear before the king for the last thirty days." ¹² Esther's response was reported to Mordecai.

¹³ Mordecai told the messenger to reply to Esther, "Don't think that you will escape the fate of all the Jews because you are in the king's palace. ¹⁴ If you keep silent at this time, relief and deliverance will come to the Jewish people from another place, but you and your father's family will be destroyed. Who knows, perhaps you have come to your royal position for such a time as this."

¹⁵ Esther sent this reply to Mordecai: ¹⁶ "Go and assemble all the Jews who can be found in Susa and fast for me. Don't eat or drink for three days, night or day. I and my female servants will also fast in the same way. After that, I will go to the king even if it is against the law. If I perish, I perish." ¹⁷ So Mordecai went and did everything Esther had commanded him.

Genesis 37:33–35

³³ His father recognized it. "It is my son's robe," he said. "A vicious animal has devoured him. Joseph has been torn to pieces!" ³⁴ Then Jacob tore his clothes, put sackcloth around his waist, and mourned for his son many days. ³⁵ All his sons and daughters tried to comfort him, but he refused to be comforted. "No," he said. "I will go down to Sheol to my son, mourning." And his father wept for him.

Romans 5:6–11
THE JUSTIFIED ARE RECONCILED

⁶ For while we were still helpless, at the right time, Christ died for the ungodly. ⁷ For rarely will someone die for a just person—though for a good person perhaps someone might even dare to die.

8 But God proves His own love for us in that while we were still sinners, Christ died for us.

⁹ How much more then, since we have now been justified by his blood, will we be saved through him from wrath. ¹⁰ For if, while we were enemies, we were reconciled to God through the death of his Son, then how much more, having been reconciled, will we be saved by his life. ¹¹ And not only that, but we also boast in God through our Lord Jesus Christ, through whom we have now received this reconciliation.

4

REFLECTION QUESTIONS

◇ What reversals of fortune or "coincidences" occur in today's reading?

◇ How was God at work in these events?

◇ When you look back over the past year, where do you see God at work? Write a prayer asking God to help you see His presence and provision in your story.

Reversals in Esther

The book of Esther is filled with reversals of fortune. Powerless people are rescued from evil rulers. The lowly are delivered from wicked plans. Those who trust in their own glory are humbled, while the humble are exalted. The following page features a chart of the many reversals that appear in this historical account.

Reversals in Esther

King Ahasuerus is introduced as powerful, extravagant, merry, and pompous. 1:1–8

THE TWO FACES OF THE KING

The king is embarrassed and angered when Vashti refuses to come to him. 1:12

Vashti fails to appear when summoned by her king. 1:12

THE TWO QUEENS

Esther appears before the king, uninvited. 5:1–2; 8:3

Esther is introduced as an orphan under the care of her cousin Mordecai. 2:5–7

ESTHER'S PLACE IN SOCIETY

Esther is named the queen of Persia. 2:15–18

Haman demands that Mordecai bow before him in worship. 3:1–2

BOWING DOWN

Haman bows before Esther, pleading for mercy. 7:7–8

Haman plans to execute Mordecai for his character. 3:2–5; 5:14

MORDECAI'S FATE

The king honors Mordecai for his character. 8:15

Haman wants to destroy the Jewish population in Persia. 3:8–11

HAMAN'S ANNIHILATION

After Haman is put to death, his house is given to two Jewish people—Esther and Mordecai. 8:1–2

Haman builds a gallows on which to hang Mordecai. 5:9–14

HAMAN'S GALLOWS

The king has Haman hanged for treachery on the gallows Haman built. 7:10

© 2020 She Reads Truth. All rights reserved.

ESTHER 5
ESTHER APPROACHES THE KING

1 On the third day, Esther dressed in her royal clothing and stood in the inner courtyard of the palace facing it. The king was sitting on his royal throne in the royal courtroom, facing its entrance. 2 As soon as the king saw Queen Esther standing in the courtyard, she gained favor with him. The king extended the gold scepter in his hand toward Esther, and she approached and touched the tip of the scepter.

3 "What is it, Queen Esther?" the king asked her. "Whatever you want, even to half the kingdom, will be given to you."

4 "If it pleases the king," Esther replied, "may the king and Haman come today to the banquet I have prepared for them."

5 The king said, "Hurry, and get Haman so we can do as Esther has requested." So the king and Haman went to the banquet Esther had prepared.

6 While drinking the wine, the king asked Esther, "Whatever you ask will be given to you. Whatever you want, even to half the kingdom, will be done."

7 Esther answered, "This is my petition and my request: 8 If I have found favor in the eyes of the king, and if it pleases the king to grant my petition and perform my request, may the king and Haman come to the banquet I will prepare for them. Tomorrow I will do what the king has asked."

9 That day Haman left full of joy and in good spirits. But when Haman saw Mordecai at the King's Gate, and Mordecai didn't rise or tremble in fear at his presence, Haman was filled with rage toward Mordecai. 10 Yet Haman controlled himself and went home. He sent for his friends and his wife Zeresh to join him. 11 Then Haman described for them his glorious wealth and his many sons. He told them all how the king had honored him and promoted him in rank over the other officials and the royal staff. 12 "What's more," Haman added, "Queen Esther invited no one but me to join the king at the banquet she had prepared. I am invited again tomorrow to join her with the king. 13 Still, none of this satisfies me since I see Mordecai the Jew sitting at the King's Gate all the time."

14 His wife Zeresh and all his friends told him, "Have them build a gallows seventy-five feet tall. Ask the king in the morning to hang Mordecai on it. Then go to the banquet with the king and enjoy yourself." The advice pleased Haman, so he had the gallows constructed.

Proverbs 16:18

Pride comes before destruction,
and an arrogant spirit before a fall.

Mark 6:14–29
JOHN THE BAPTIST BEHEADED

[14] King Herod heard about it, because Jesus's name had become well known. Some said, "John the Baptist has been raised from the dead, and that's why miraculous powers are at work in him." [15] But others said, "He's Elijah." Still others said, "He's a prophet, like one of the prophets from long ago."

[16] When Herod heard of it, he said, "John, the one I beheaded, has been raised!"

[17] For Herod himself had given orders to arrest John and to chain him in prison on account of Herodias, his brother Philip's wife, because he had married her. [18] John had been telling Herod, "It is not lawful for you to have your brother's wife." [19] So Herodias held a grudge against him and wanted to kill him. But she could not, [20] because Herod feared John and protected him, knowing he was a righteous and holy man. When Herod heard him he would be very perplexed, and yet he liked to listen to him.

[21] An opportune time came on his birthday, when Herod gave a banquet for his nobles, military commanders, and the leading men of Galilee. [22] When Herodias's own daughter came in and danced, she pleased Herod and his guests. The king said to the girl, "Ask me whatever you want, and I'll give it to you." [23] He promised her with an oath: "Whatever you ask me I will give you, up to half my kingdom."

[24] She went out and said to her mother, "What should I ask for?"

"John the Baptist's head," she said.

[25] At once she hurried to the king and said, "I want you to give me John the Baptist's head on a platter immediately." [26] Although the king was deeply distressed, because of his oaths and the guests he did not want to refuse her. [27] The king immediately sent for an executioner and commanded him to bring John's head. So he went and beheaded him in prison, [28] brought his head on a platter, and gave it to the girl. Then the girl gave it to her mother. [29] When John's disciples heard about it, they came and removed his corpse and placed it in a tomb.

5

REFLECTION QUESTIONS

◇ What reversals
of fortune or
"coincidences" occur
in today's reading?

◇ How was God
at work in
these events?

◇ When you look back
over the past month,
where do you see
God at work? Write
a prayer asking God
to help you see
His presence and
provision in your
daily life.

GRACE DAY
GRACE DAY
GRACE DAY

GRACE DAY
GRACE DAY
GRACE DAY

6

Take this day to catch
up on your reading,
pray, and rest in the
presence of the Lord.

◇   ◇   ◇

YOU are MY HIDING
PLACE; YOU PROTECT
ME FROM TROUBLE.
YOU SURROUND ME
WITH JOYFUL SHOUTS
OF DELIVERANCE.

PSALM 32:7

◇   ◇   ◇

Scripture is God-breathed and true. When we memorize it, we carry His Word with us wherever we go.

During this reading plan, we will commit Esther 4:14 to memory. Read through the verse out loud a few times. Vary the way you say it, each time placing the emphasis on different words or phrases to help you remember what is happening. This week, focus on memorizing just the first half.

7

If you keep silent at this time,
relief and deliverance will
come to the Jewish people
from another place, but you
and your father's family will be
destroyed. Who knows, perhaps
you have come to your royal
position for such a time as this.

ESTHER 4:14

EIGHT

DAY

MORDECAI HONORED
BY THE KING

MORDECAI HONORED
BY THE KING

ESTHER 6
MORDECAI HONORED BY THE KING

¹ That night sleep escaped the king, so he ordered the book recording daily events to be brought and read to the king. ² They found the written report of how Mordecai had informed on Bigthana and Teresh, two of the king's eunuchs who guarded the entrance, when they planned to assassinate King Ahasuerus. ³ The king inquired, "What honor and special recognition have been given to Mordecai for this act?"

The king's personal attendants replied, "Nothing has been done for him."

⁴ The king asked, "Who is in the court?" Now Haman was just entering the outer court of the palace to ask the king to hang Mordecai on the gallows he had prepared for him.

⁵ The king's attendants answered him, "Haman is there, standing in the court."

"Have him enter," the king ordered. ⁶ Haman entered, and the king asked him,

"WHAT SHOULD BE DONE FOR THE MAN THE KING WANTS TO HONOR?"

Haman thought to himself, "Who is it the king would want to honor more than me?" ⁷ Haman told the king, "For the man the king wants to honor: ⁸ Have them bring a royal garment that the king himself has worn and a horse the king himself has ridden, which has a royal crown on its head. ⁹ Put the garment and the horse under the charge of one of the king's most noble officials. Have them clothe the man the king wants to honor, parade him on the horse through the city square, and call out before him, 'This is what is done for the man the king wants to honor.'"

¹⁰ The king told Haman, "Hurry, and do just as you proposed. Take a garment and a horse for Mordecai the Jew, who is sitting at the King's Gate. Do not leave out anything you have suggested."

¹¹ So Haman took the garment and the horse. He clothed Mordecai and paraded him through the city square, calling out before him, "This is what is done for the man the king wants to honor."

¹² Then Mordecai returned to the King's Gate, but Haman hurried off for home, mournful and with his head covered. ¹³ Haman told his wife Zeresh and all his

friends everything that had happened. His advisers and his wife Zeresh said to him, "Since Mordecai is Jewish, and you have begun to fall before him, you won't overcome him, because your downfall is certain." ¹⁴ While they were still speaking with him, the king's eunuchs arrived and rushed Haman to the banquet Esther had prepared.

PROVERBS 26:27
The one who digs a pit will fall into it,
and whoever rolls a stone—
it will come back on him.

ISAIAH 52:1-2, 7-10
¹ Wake up, wake up;
put on your strength, Zion!
Put on your beautiful garments,
Jerusalem, the holy city!
For the uncircumcised and the unclean
will no longer enter you.
² Stand up, shake the dust off yourself!
Take your seat, Jerusalem.
Remove the bonds from your neck,
captive Daughter Zion.

…

⁷ HOW Beautiful on
the mountains
are the feet of the
Herald,
WHO Proclaims
Peace,
WHO Brings news of
Good things,

who proclaims salvation,
who says to Zion, "Your God reigns!"
⁸ The voices of your watchmen—
they lift up their voices,
shouting for joy together;
for every eye will see
when the LORD returns to Zion.
⁹ Be joyful, rejoice together,
you ruins of Jerusalem!

FOR the LORD has
comforted HIS
People;
He has redeemed
Jerusalem.

¹⁰ The LORD has displayed his holy arm
in the sight of all the nations;
all the ends of the earth will see
the salvation of our God.

REFLECTION QUESTIONS

◇ What reversals
of fortune or
"coincidences" occur
in today's reading?

◇ How was God
at work in
these events?

◇ Where do you see
God at work in your
friendships? Write a
prayer asking God
to help you see His
presence and provision
in your friendships.

SPIRITUAL RHYTHMS IN THE BOOK OF ESTHER

The book of Esther shows examples of the Jewish people practicing rhythms of lament, fasting, rest, celebration, and remembrance in their daily lives. These rhythms, practiced by Jesus and His disciples as well as Christians today, remind God's people of His presence and past provision and point to His future work.

The following pages present a summary of how and where each of these five rhythms are practiced in the book of Esther.

LAMENT

◇ Mordecai laments Haman's plot to kill the Jewish people by tearing his clothes, putting on sackcloth and ashes, and crying loudly in the city.
4:1-2

◇ The Jewish people also mourn the news of Haman's plot.
4:3

FASTING

◇ The Jewish people fast after hearing about Haman's plot to kill them.
4:3

◇ Esther asks Mordecai and the Jewish people to fast for three days and nights before she approaches King Ahasuerus. She and her female servants do the same.
4:16

REST

◇ Jewish people living in rural villages rest on the fourteenth day of the month of Adar after defeating their enemies.
9:17

◇ Jewish people living in Susa rest on the fifteenth day of the month of Adar after defeating their enemies.
9:18

CeLeBRaTion

◇ Days fourteen and
fifteen in the month
of Adar become days
of feasting and
rejoicing, and Purim
is established as a
holiday in the Jewish
calendar celebrating
the Jewish people's
survival and their
enemy's demise.

ReMeMBRance

◇ The Jewish people
commit to observing
Purim yearly in order
to honor and preserve
the memory of their
deliverance for
future generations.

© 2020 She Reads Truth. All rights reserved.

DAY NINE

HAMAN IS EXECUTED

◇   ◇   ◇   ◇   ◇   ◇

ESTHER 7
HAMAN IS EXECUTED

¹ The king and Haman came to feast with Esther the queen. ² Once again, on the second day while drinking wine, the king asked Esther, "Queen Esther, whatever you ask will be given to you. Whatever you seek, even to half the kingdom, will be done."

³ Queen Esther answered, "If I have found favor with you, Your Majesty, and if the king is pleased, spare my life; this is my request. And spare my people; this is my desire. ⁴ For my people and I have been sold to destruction, death, and annihilation. If we had merely been sold as male and female slaves, I would have kept silent. Indeed, the trouble wouldn't be worth burdening the king."

⁵ King Ahasuerus spoke up and asked Queen Esther, "Who is this, and where is the one who would devise such a scheme?"

⁶ Esther answered, "The adversary and enemy is this evil Haman."

Haman stood terrified before the king and queen. ⁷ The king arose in anger and went from where they were drinking wine to the palace garden. Haman remained to beg Queen Esther for his life because he realized the king was planning something terrible for him. ⁸ Just as the king returned from the palace garden to the banquet hall, Haman was falling on the couch where Esther was reclining. The king exclaimed, "Would he actually violate the queen while I am in the house?" As soon as the statement left the king's mouth, they covered Haman's face.

⁹ Harbona, one of the king's eunuchs, said, "There is a gallows seventy-five feet tall at Haman's house that he made for Mordecai, who gave the report that saved the king."

The king said, "Hang him on it."

¹⁰ They hanged Haman on the gallows he had prepared for Mordecai. Then the king's anger subsided.

PSALM 91:2-3

² I will say concerning the
Lord, who is my refuge and my fortress,
my god in whom I trust:
³ He himself will rescue you from the bird trap,
from the destructive plague.

REVELATION 20:11-15
THE GREAT WHITE THRONE JUDGMENT

¹¹ Then I saw a great white throne and one seated on it. Earth and heaven fled from his presence, and no place was found for them.

¹² I ALSO SAW THE DEAD, THE GREAT AND THE SMALL, STANDING BEFORE THE THRONE, AND BOOKS WERE OPENED. ANOTHER BOOK WAS OPENED, WHICH IS THE BOOK OF LIFE, AND THE DEAD WERE JUDGED ACCORDING TO THEIR WORKS BY WHAT WAS WRITTEN IN THE BOOKS.

¹³ Then the sea gave up the dead that were in it, and death and Hades gave up the dead that were in them; each one was judged according to their works. ¹⁴ Death and Hades were thrown into the lake of fire. This is the second death, the lake of fire. ¹⁵ And anyone whose name was not found written in the book of life was thrown into the lake of fire.

9

REFLECTION QUESTIONS

◇ What reversals of fortune or "coincidences" occur in today's reading?

◇ How was God at work in these events?

◇ Where do you see God at work in your family? Write a prayer asking God to help you see His presence and provision in your family.

ESTHER INTERVENES
FOR THE JEWS

DAY

TEN

FOR THE JEWS
ESTHER INTERVENES

ESTHER 8
ESTHER INTERVENES FOR THE JEWS

¹ That same day King Ahasuerus awarded Queen Esther the estate of Haman, the enemy of the Jews. Mordecai entered the king's presence because Esther had revealed her relationship to Mordecai. ² The king removed his signet ring he had recovered from Haman and gave it to Mordecai, and Esther put him in charge of Haman's estate.

³ Then Esther addressed the king again. She fell at his feet, wept, and begged him to revoke the evil of Haman the Agagite and his plot he had devised against the Jews. ⁴ The king extended the gold scepter toward Esther, so she got up and stood before the king.

⁵ She said, "If it pleases the king and I have found favor with him, if the matter seems right to the king and I am pleasing in his eyes, let a royal edict be written. Let it revoke the documents the scheming Haman son of Hammedatha the Agagite wrote to destroy the Jews who are in all the king's provinces. ⁶ For how could I bear to see the disaster that would come on my people? How could I bear to see the destruction of my relatives?"

⁷ King Ahasuerus said to Esther the queen and to Mordecai the Jew, "Look, I have given Haman's estate to Esther, and he was hanged on the gallows because he attacked the Jews. ⁸ Write in the king's name whatever pleases you concerning the Jews, and seal it with the royal signet ring. A document written in the king's name and sealed with the royal signet ring cannot be revoked."

⁹ On the twenty-third day of the third month—that is, the month Sivan—the royal scribes were summoned. Everything was written exactly as Mordecai commanded for the Jews, to the satraps, the governors, and the officials of the 127 provinces from India to Cush. The edict was written for each province in its own script, for each ethnic group in its own language, and to the Jews in their own script and language.

¹⁰ Mordecai wrote in King Ahasuerus's name and sealed the edicts with the royal signet ring. He sent the documents by mounted couriers, who rode fast horses bred in the royal stables.

[11] The king's edict gave the Jews in each and every city the right to assemble and defend themselves, to destroy, kill, and annihilate every ethnic and provincial army hostile to them, including women and children, and to take their possessions as spoils of war. [12] This would take place on a single day throughout all the provinces of King Ahasuerus, on the thirteenth day of the twelfth month, the month Adar.

[13] A copy of the text, issued as law throughout every province, was distributed to all the peoples so the Jews could be ready to avenge themselves against their enemies on that day. [14] The couriers rode out in haste on their royal horses at the king's urgent command. The law was also issued in the fortress of Susa.

[15] Mordecai went from the king's presence clothed in royal blue and white, with a great gold crown and a purple robe of fine linen. The city of Susa shouted and rejoiced, [16] and the Jews celebrated with gladness, joy, and honor. [17] In every province and every city where the king's command and edict reached, gladness and joy took place among the Jews. There was a celebration and a holiday. And many of the ethnic groups of the land professed themselves to be Jews because fear of the Jews had overcome them.

ROMANS 8:10-11

[10] Now if Christ is in you, the body is dead because of sin, but the Spirit gives life because of righteousness. [11] And if the Spirit of him who raised Jesus from the dead lives in you, then he who raised Christ from the dead will also bring your mortal bodies to life through his Spirit who lives in you.

COLOSSIANS 3:1-4
THE LIFE OF THE NEW MAN

[1] So if you have been raised with Christ, seek the things above, where Christ is, seated at the right hand of God. [2] Set your minds on things above, not on earthly things. [3] For you died, and your life is hidden with Christ in God. [4] When Christ, who is your life, appears, then you also will appear with him in glory.

10

REFLECTION QUESTIONS

◇ What reversals of fortune or "coincidences" occur in today's reading?

◇ How was God at work in these events?

◇ Where do you see God at work in your church? Write a prayer asking God to help you see His presence and provision in your church.

DAY ELEVEN

THE VICTORIES OF THE JEWS

◇   ◇   ◇   ◇   ◇   ◇

ESTHER 9:1–22
VICTORIES OF THE JEWS

¹ The king's command and law went into effect on the thirteenth day of the twelfth month, the month Adar.

ON THE DAY WHEN THE JEWS' ENEMIES HAD HOPED TO OVERPOWER THEM, JUST THE OPPOSITE HAPPENED.

The Jews overpowered those who hated them. ² In each of King Ahasuerus's provinces the Jews assembled in their cities to attack those who intended to harm them. Not a single person could withstand them; fear of them fell on every nationality.

³ All the officials of the provinces, the satraps, the governors, and the royal civil administrators aided the Jews because they feared Mordecai. ⁴ For Mordecai exercised great power in the palace, and his fame spread throughout the provinces as he became more and more powerful.

⁵ The Jews put all their enemies to the sword, killing and destroying them. They did what they pleased to those who hated them. ⁶ In the fortress of Susa the Jews killed and destroyed five hundred men, ⁷ including Parshandatha, Dalphon, Aspatha, ⁸ Poratha, Adalia, Aridatha, ⁹ Parmashta, Arisai, Aridai, and Vaizatha. ¹⁰ They killed these ten sons of Haman son of Hammedatha, the enemy of the Jews. However, they did not seize any plunder.

¹¹ On that day the number of people killed in the fortress of Susa was reported to the king. ¹² The king said to Queen Esther, "In the fortress of Susa the Jews have killed and destroyed five hundred men, including Haman's ten sons. What have they done in the rest of the royal provinces? Whatever you ask will be given to you. Whatever you seek will also be done."

¹³ Esther answered, "If it pleases the king, may the Jews who are in Susa also have tomorrow to carry out today's law, and may the bodies of Haman's ten sons be hung on the gallows." ¹⁴ The king gave the orders for this to be done, so a law was announced in Susa, and they hung the bodies of Haman's ten sons. ¹⁵ The Jews in Susa assembled again on the fourteenth day of the month of Adar and killed three hundred men in Susa, but they did not seize any plunder.

¹⁶ The rest of the Jews in the royal provinces assembled, defended themselves, and gained relief from their enemies. They killed seventy-five thousand of those who hated them, but they did not seize any plunder. ¹⁷ They fought on the thirteenth day of the month of Adar and rested on the fourteenth, and it became a day of feasting and rejoicing.

¹⁸ But the Jews in Susa had assembled on the thirteenth and the fourteenth days of the month. They rested on the fifteenth day of the month, and it became a day of feasting and rejoicing. ¹⁹ This explains why the rural Jews who live in villages observe the fourteenth day of the month of Adar as a time of rejoicing and feasting. It is a holiday when they send gifts to one another.

²⁰ Mordecai recorded these events and sent letters to all the Jews in all of King Ahasuerus's provinces, both near and far. ²¹ He ordered them to celebrate the fourteenth and fifteenth days of the month of Adar every year ²² because during those days the Jews gained relief from their enemies. That was the month when their sorrow was turned into rejoicing and their mourning into a holiday. They were to be days of feasting, rejoicing, and of sending gifts to one another and to the poor.

NEHEMIAH 8:10

Then he said to them, "Go and eat what is rich, drink what is sweet, and send portions to those who have nothing prepared, since today is holy to our Lord. Do not grieve, because the joy of the LORD is your strength."

LUKE 1:46–55
MARY'S PRAISE

⁴⁶ And Mary said:

My soul magnifies the Lord,
⁴⁷ and my spirit rejoices in God my Savior,
⁴⁸ because he has looked with favor
on the humble condition of his servant.
Surely, from now on all generations
will call me blessed,
⁴⁹ because the Mighty One
has done great things for me,
and his name is holy.
⁵⁰ His mercy is from generation to generation
on those who fear him.
⁵¹ He has done a mighty deed with his arm;
he has scattered the proud
because of the thoughts of their hearts;
⁵² he has toppled the mighty from their thrones
and exalted the lowly.
⁵³ He has satisfied the hungry with good things
and sent the rich away empty.
⁵⁴ He has helped his servant Israel,
remembering his mercy
⁵⁵ to Abraham and his descendants forever,
just as he spoke to our ancestors.

11

REFLECTION QUESTIONS

◇ What reversals
of fortune or
"coincidences" occur
in today's reading?

◇ How was God
at work in
these events?

◇ Where do you see
God at work in your
community? Write
a prayer asking God
to help you see His
presence and provision
in your community.

MORDECAI'S FAME

DAY

TWELVE

MORDECAI'S FAME

ESTHER 9:23-32

²³ So the Jews agreed to continue the practice they had begun, as Mordecai had written them to do. ²⁴ For Haman son of Hammedatha the Agagite, the enemy of all the Jews, had plotted against the Jews to destroy them. He cast the pur—that is, the lot—to crush and destroy them. ²⁵ But when the matter was brought before the king, he commanded by letter that the evil plan Haman had devised against the Jews return on his own head and that he should be hanged with his sons on the gallows. ²⁶ For this reason these days are called Purim, from the word pur. Because of all the instructions in this letter as well as what they had witnessed and what had happened to them, ²⁷ the Jews bound themselves, their descendants, and all who joined with them to a commitment that they would not fail to celebrate these two days each and every year according to the written instructions and according to the time appointed. ²⁸ These days are remembered and celebrated by every generation, family, province, and city, so that these days of Purim will not lose their significance in Jewish life and their memory will not fade from their descendants.

²⁹ Queen Esther, daughter of Abihail, along with Mordecai the Jew, wrote this second letter with full authority to confirm the letter about Purim. ³⁰ He sent letters with assurances of peace and security to all the Jews who were in the 127 provinces of the kingdom of Ahasuerus, ³¹ in order to confirm these days of Purim at their proper time just as Mordecai the Jew and Esther the queen had established them and just as they had committed themselves and their descendants to the practices of fasting and lamentation. ³² So Esther's command confirmed these customs of Purim, which were then written into the record.

ESTHER 10
MORDECAI'S FAME

¹ King Ahasuerus imposed a tax throughout the land even to the farthest shores. ² All of his powerful and magnificent accomplishments and the detailed account of Mordecai's great rank with which the king had honored him, have they not been written in the Book of the Historical Events of the Kings of Media and Persia? ³ Mordecai the Jew was second only to King Ahasuerus. He was famous among the Jews and highly esteemed by many of his relatives. He continued to pursue prosperity for his people and to speak for the well-being of all his descendants.

LEVITICUS 16:29-31

²⁹ "This is to be a permanent statute for you: In the seventh month, on the tenth day of the month you are to practice self-denial and do no work, both the native and the alien who resides among you. ³⁰ Atonement will be made for you on this

day to cleanse you, and you will be clean from all your sins before the Lᴏʀᴅ. ³¹ It is a Sabbath of complete rest for you, and you must practice self-denial; it is a permanent statute."

EPHESIANS 1:3–14
GOD'S RICH BLESSINGS

³ Blessed is the God and Father of our Lord Jesus Christ, who has blessed us with every spiritual blessing in the heavens in Christ. ⁴ For he chose us in him, before the foundation of the world, to be holy and blameless in love before him. ⁵ He predestined us to be adopted as sons through Jesus Christ for himself, according to the good pleasure of his will, ⁶ to the praise of his glorious grace that he lavished on us in the Beloved One.

⁷ In him we have redemption through his blood, the forgiveness of our trespasses, according to the riches of his grace ⁸ that he richly poured out on us with all wisdom and understanding.

⁹ HE MADE KNOWN TO US THE MYSTERY OF HIS WILL, ACCORDING TO HIS GOOD PLEASURE THAT HE PURPOSED IN CHRIST ¹⁰ AS A PLAN FOR THE RIGHT TIME—TO BRING EVERYTHING TOGETHER IN CHRIST, BOTH THINGS IN HEAVEN AND THINGS ON EARTH IN HIM.

¹¹ In him we have also received an inheritance, because we were predestined according to the plan of the one who works out everything in agreement with the purpose of his will, ¹² so that we who had already put our hope in Christ might bring praise to his glory.

¹³ In him you also were sealed with the promised Holy Spirit when you heard the word of truth, the gospel of your salvation, and when you believed. ¹⁴ The Holy Spirit is the down payment of our inheritance, until the redemption of the possession, to the praise of his glory.

12

REFLECTION QUESTIONS

◇ What reversals
of fortune or
"coincidences" occur
in today's reading?

◇ How was God
at work in
these events?

◇ Where do you see
God at work in your
heart? Write a prayer
asking God to help
you see His Spirit at
work in your heart.

OLD Testament Festivals Fulfilled in Christ

The Jewish festival of Purim originates in Esther 9:20-28. Also known as the Festival of Lots, it celebrates the Jewish people's deliverance from Haman's plan to destroy them in Persia.

Purim and other Jewish festivals commemorate what it means for a people to belong to the Lord. The festivals help God's people recall His faithfulness—a faithfulness ultimately fulfilled in Christ. This chart provides a look at what each festival celebrates, how Christ fulfills them, and when each occurs.*

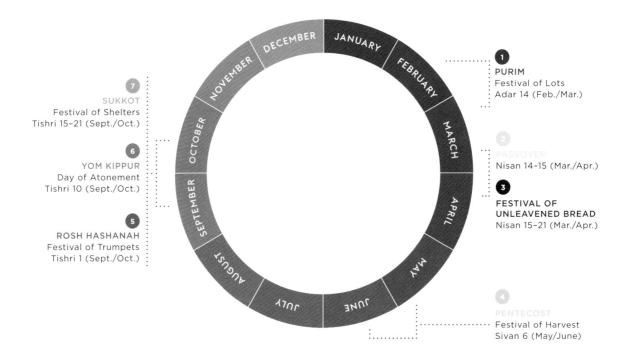

7 SUKKOT
Festival of Shelters
Tishri 15–21 (Sept./Oct.)

6 YOM KIPPUR
Day of Atonement
Tishri 10 (Sept./Oct.)

5 ROSH HASHANAH
Festival of Trumpets
Tishri 1 (Sept./Oct.)

1 PURIM
Festival of Lots
Adar 14 (Feb./Mar.)

2 PASSOVER
Nisan 14–15 (Mar./Apr.)

3 FESTIVAL OF UNLEAVENED BREAD
Nisan 15–21 (Mar./Apr.)

4 PENTECOST
Festival of Harvest
Sivan 6 (May/June)

Festival dates are given in the Hebrew calendar along with the months where they usually fall.

© 2020 She Reads Truth. All rights reserved.

FESTIVAL DESCRIPTION	FULFILLED IN CHRIST

 PURIM

Commemorates how the Jewish people were delivered from Haman's plot to kill them in the days of Esther.
EST 9

We would have perished in our sin without Christ's intervention. As Esther represented her people by pleading their case before the Persian king, Jesus represents us before God.
JN 3:16-17; 2CO 1:9-11; 2TM 4:18; HEB 13:6

 PASSOVER

Commemorates how God spared the firstborn sons of Israel in Egypt, accepting the blood of a lamb instead.

Christ, God's firstborn Son, became our Passover Lamb by dying in our place.

 FESTIVAL OF UNLEAVENED BREAD

Commemorates God's deliverance of Israel out of Egypt. In their haste to flee, they had no time to let their bread leaven.
EX 12:39-42; LV 23:6-8

Christ instituted the Lord's Supper on the eve of this festival, breaking bread and calling it His body, given for His people. During this festival, He was buried, like a seed waiting to bear the first fruit of salvation.
MK 14:1; 1CO 5:6-8

 PENTECOST

Commemorates the giving of the law at Mount Sinai. It was meant to be a guide for life, but because of sin, no one could live a life of complete obedience.

Christ's resurrection made Him the "firstfruits from the dead," the one who kept the law perfectly in our place. After His resurrection, He sent the Holy Spirit to live within His people and bear spiritual fruit in us.

 ROSH HASHANAH

Celebrates the beginning of a new year with the blowing of trumpets. This festival reminded God's people of His faithful love for them.
LV 23:23-25; NM 10:9; 29:1-6

The return of Christ will happen at the sound of a heavenly trumpet. That day will mark a new beginning as He ushers in His kingdom perfectly and completely.
MT 24:30-31; 1CO 15:51-52; 1TH 4:16

 YOM KIPPUR

The day the high priest makes atonement for the nation's sin before God. The sins of the nation were symbolically placed on a goat which was cast out of the camp.
EX 30:10; LV 16:15-27; 23:26-33

Jesus was led to a cross outside the city walls, like the goat cast outside of the camp. On the cross, He bore our sins, sanctifying us by His blood.
IS 53:1-12; HEB 13:11-12; RV 13:8

 SUKKOT

Commemorates Israel's forty years of wilderness wandering. God dwelt among His people in the tabernacle, giving them manna and water.
LV 23:33-43; NM 29:12-39; DT 16:13

Jesus is God who took on flesh and dwelled among us. He gives us all we need to live eternally.
JN 1:10-14; HEB 9:1-11

GRACE DAY GRACE DAY

GRACE DAY

GRACE DAY

13

Take this day to catch
up on your reading,
pray, and rest in the
presence of the Lord.

GRACE DAY

GRACE DAY

GRACE DAY GRACE DAY

◇   ◇   ◇

BLESSED IS THE GOD AND
FATHER OF OUR LORD
JESUS CHRIST, WHO HAS
BLESSED US WITH EVERY
SPIRITUAL BLESSING IN
THE HEAVENS IN CHRIST.

EPHESIANS 1:3

◇   ◇   ◇

Scripture is God-breathed and true. When we memorize it, we carry
His Word with us wherever we go.

This week, we will memorize the last half of Esther 4:14. Continue
reading the full verse out loud multiple times, and practice your
memorization by copying it in the space provided.

DAY   14

IF YOU KEEP SILENT AT THIS TIME,
RELIEF AND DELIVERANCE WILL
COME TO THE JEWISH PEOPLE
FROM ANOTHER PLACE, BUT YOU
AND YOUR FATHER'S FAMILY WILL BE
DESTROYED. WHO KNOWS, PERHAPS
YOU HAVE COME TO YOUR ROYAL
POSITION FOR SUCH A TIME AS THIS.

ESTHER 4:14

NOTES

BENEDICTION

BENEDICTION

PRAISED ARE YOU,
LORD OUR GOD, WHO
SAVES HIS PEOPLE
ISRAEL FROM ALL THEIR
ENEMIES, FOR YOU ARE A
REMEMBERING GOD.

TRADITIONAL PURIM BLESSING

CSB BOOK ABBREVIATIONS

OLD TESTAMENT

GN Genesis

EX Exodus

LV Leviticus

NM Numbers

DT Deuteronomy

JOS Joshua

JDG Judges

RU Ruth

1SM 1 Samuel

2SM 2 Samuel

1KG 1 Kings

2KG 2 Kings

1CH 1 Chronicles

2CH 2 Chronicles

EZR Ezra

NEH Nehemiah

EST Esther

JB Job

PS Psalms

PR Proverbs

EC Ecclesiastes

SG Song of Solomon

IS Isaiah

JR Jeremiah

LM Lamentations

EZK Ezekiel

DN Daniel

HS Hosea

JL Joel

AM Amos

OB Obadiah

JNH Jonah

MC Micah

NAH Nahum

HAB Habakkuk

ZPH Zephaniah

HG Haggai

ZCH Zechariah

MAL Malachi

NEW TESTAMENT

MT Matthew

MK Mark

LK Luke

JN John

AC Acts

RM Romans

1CO 1 Corinthians

2CO 2 Corinthians

GL Galatians

EPH Ephesians

PHP Philippians

COL Colossians

1TH 1 Thessalonians

2TH 2 Thessalonians

1TM 1 Timothy

2TM 2 Timothy

TI Titus

PHM Philemon

HEB Hebrews

JMS James

1PT 1 Peter

2PT 2 Peter

1JN 1 John

2JN 2 John

3JN 3 John

JD Jude

RV Revelation

BIBLIOGRAPHY

Linafelt, T. "Purim." *Eerdmans Dictionary of the Bible*, (2000): 1100.

Strassfeld, Michael. *The Jewish Holidays: A Guide & Commentary.* New York City: William Morrow Paperbacks, 2001.

SHE READS TRUTH | BIBLE

Inspired by the She Reads Truth mission of "Women in the Word of God every day," the *She Reads Truth Bible* is thoughtfully and artfully designed to highlight the beauty, goodness, and truth found in Scripture.

FEATURES

- Custom reading plans to help you navigate your time in the Word

- Thoughtful devotionals throughout each book of the Bible

- Maps, charts, and timelines to provide context and Scripture connections

- 66 hand-lettered key verses to aid in Scripture memorization

USE CODE SRTB15 FOR 15% OFF YOUR
NEW SHE READS TRUTH BIBLE!

SHOPSHEREADSTRUTH.COM

Like everything we do at She Reads Truth, our podcast supports one simple but powerful mission: women in the Word of God every day.

Our hope is that this podcast will serve as a complement to every reading plan, to encourage you on your commute to work, while you're out for a walk, or at home making dinner. God's Word is for you and for now. Join our founders Raechel and Amanda in a conversation that looks at the beauty, goodness, and truth found in Scripture. Subscribe to the podcast today and make it a part of your week!

SHE READS TRUTH

PODCAST

Love Letters & Light in the Darkness
She Reads Truth Podcast — Apr 13, 20

1×

JOIN US ON APPLE PODCASTS OR YOUR
PREFERRED STREAMING PLATFORM.

WHERE DID I STUDY?

O HOME
O OFFICE
O COFFEE SHOP
O CHURCH
O A FRIEND'S HOUSE
O OTHER:

WHAT WAS I LISTENING TO?

ARTIST:

SONG:

PLAYLIST:

WHEN DID I STUDY?

MORNING

AFTERNOON

NIGHT

HOW DID I FIND DELIGHT IN GOD'S WORD?

WHAT WAS HAPPENING IN MY LIFE?

WHAT WAS HAPPENING IN THE WORLD?

MONTH	DAY	YEAR

END DATE